THE INDUSTRY

OF THE

FREEDMEN OF AMERICA.

PART I.—CHIEFLY AS SHOWN BY THOSE EMANCIPATED BEFORE THE WAR.

PART II.—AS PROMOTED BY THE AMERICAN FREEDMEN'S UNION COMMISSION, AND OTHER KINDRED ASSOCIATIONS.

ISSUED AND PUBLISHED BY

THE NATIONAL FREEDMEN'S AID UNION:

SIR T. F. BUXTON, BART., M.P., *President*.
A. HAMPSON, *Secretary*, 12, Bishopsgate Without, London.

E
185.2
.N28

PART I.

EXTRACTS
FROM THE REPORTS OF
THE FREEDMEN'S INQUIRY COMMISSION,
AND OTHER AUTHORITIES,
DEMONSTRATIVE OF THE INDUSTRIOUS AND SELF-SUSTAINING ABILITY OF THE FREE PEOPLE OF COLOUR IN THE UNITED STATES.

The Freedmen's Inquiry Commission was appointed by President Lincoln. It has presented two reports, which are models of exhaustive research and well-classified information.

Dr. Howe, one of those Commissioners, as the educator of Laura Bridgman, the celebrated blind, deaf, and dumb girl, and from other causes, has an European reputation.

1.—"In the city of Washington, containing sixteen thousand free coloured persons, the free coloured people support their own poor without alms-house aid, and scarcely a beggar is found among them."—*Freedmen's Inquiry Commission Report, p. 3.*

2.—Mrs. Daniel Breed, "an intelligent lady, wife of a physician in Washington, deposed before the Commission, 'I have known but two instances of beggary by coloured people during my residence of ten years in this city. A few are supported by charity from their own churches.'"—*Idem, p. 3.*

3.—" In Alexandria, and in various other places, it came to the knowledge of the Commission that one of the first acts of the negroes, when they found themselves free, was to establish schools at their own expense."—*Idem, p.* 4.

4.—"Scarcely any beggars are found among them. Like the Quakers, they maintain their own poor. When a case occurs in which a family is unable to meet the expenses of sickness, or perhaps the cost of a funeral, it is *among themselves alone* that a subscription paper, usually called a 'pony purse,' passes in aid of the sufferers."—*Freedmen's Inquiry Commission. Report,* 1864. *p.* 100.

5.—"One hears current among slaveholders the assertion that negroes emancipated and left to themselves are worthless and helpless, and are sure in the end to become a burden on the community. But the Commission has not found in a single locality occupied by numbers of free negroes proof that there is any truth in such an opinion; on the contrary, the actual facts are all against it."—*Freedmen's Inquiry Report.*

6.—One remarkable fact has been just published from the Freedmen's Aid Bureau, viz.:—That in the State of Texas, where in 1860 there were 182,000 slaves, there are now only 67 persons receiving Government support. *(Feb.,* 1866.*)*

7.—The Commission ascertained that the free coloured people of Louisiana, in the year 1860, paid taxes on an assessment of thirteen millions. But by the census of 1860, the free coloured population of that State is put at 18,647. This would give an average for each person of about seven hundred dollars of property. But the average amount of property to each person throughout the loyal free States is estimated at four hundred and eighty-four dollars only. It follows that the free coloured people of Louisiana (even supposing their numbers to be more correctly estimated as the Commission were informed might be the case, at 25,000) are, on the average, richer by seven and a half per cent. than the people of the Northern States. And this occurs, it should be remembered, under many civil disabilities, which are a great pecuniary injury seriously restricting the means of accumulating property. —*Idem, p.* 101.

8.—Throughout the State the coloured people manage their own church affairs. A great many of the churches now owned by them had been failures in the hands of white people. The negroes bought and paid for them, and have improved them very much since the purchase.—*Idem, p.* 101.

9.—The coloured citizens of New Orleans own real estate to the value of 15,000,000 dollars, and they now have a daily newspaper, the *Tribune,* printed and edited by coloured men.—*Idem.*

10.—A Southern man, says Sir Morton Peto, made the following answer to his letter of enquiry:—" Born in Louisiana, on my father's sugar plantation near New Orleans, I have known slavery in all its phases, though

I have had no connection with it for twelve years. Two years ago, after the emancipation of the slaves, one of my father's plantations in Louisiana came into my hands. There were 150 negroes on the plantation. From that day to this I have not heard an instance of difficulty among the workmen. The gentleman who leased the property for a number of years is a Southerner, and was a very ardent Secessionist. He is also a truly Christian man. He writes me that he has had no difficulty with his workmen that was not very easily arranged by conversation. They have been paid regularly every month their full wages, their children go to school, and the work of the plantation goes on with greater alacrity than when the negroes were slaves. The same may be said of several plantations in the neighbourhood where the workmen are regularly paid and kindly treated. I have no fears for the future of the Freedmen, unless they are driven by harsh laws to array themselves against the whites."

The same writer mentions that a friend of his, Colonel Drury, who owned a large estate, only lost 3 out of 1000 labourers after freedom was granted.

11.—General Howard's Report to Congress, "that he had found them on the whole order-loving, law-abiding, and self-helpful," is specially and signally confirmed by the address which General Jenkins, Governor of Georgia, made to the Legislature of the State—appealing to it when in session—to confirm the declaration "that in the main the conduct of the negroes has been praiseworthy beyond all rational expectation; and that their fidelity in the past, and their decorum under the distressing circumstances of the present, are without a parallel in history."

As this message was delivered to an assembly mainly composed of the Planters of that State, which before the war contained 462,000, or the largest slave population of any State, and as the planters' idea of praiseworthy conduct and decorum is known to consist mainly in that of hard work, nothing can seem more conclusive than this evidence.

12.—" There is no more distress among those who have been free for a year, than among the same number of poor in Philadelphia."

13.—" The Contraband Camp in the Department of the Cumberland have this year raised 300,000 dollars worth of cotton."

" Last spring I visited the Contraband Camp at Huntsville, Ala. It contained about 300 persons, one half of whom were ill. It was entirely dependent on the Government and charity of the North. It was the scene of squalor and misery beyond description. Mark the change. But a few weeks since I visited it again—population about the same; on the sick-list *two*—camp, nearly self-supporting; and had it not been for the raid upon the plantation they would have returned to the Government all with which they were supplied last year. And these were women and children, and a few men unfit for the army."

** Statements made by Wm. Forster Mitchell, Nashville, Tennessee, a gentleman of high character, whose ability equals his benevolence. He is named after the father of Wm. E. Forster, Esq., M.P., the late Under-Secretary of the Colonies.

The following, as of recent date, and relating to Nashville and Richmond, and especially the case of the latter city, as so recently delivered from the siege and ravage of war, are wonderful evidences of high Christian citizenship, scarcely of their kind to be equalled anywhere :—

General Fisk's last official, but unpublished Report from Tennessee, states that a Provident Association has been formed at Nashville, capital of Tennessee, conducted by the coloured people, which relieves the suffering poor *without distinction of colour*, that more whites than coloured people are its beneficiaries, and that many widows and orphans whose husbands and fathers fell fighting to perpetuate slavery, have been fed and warmed through the kindly offices of " *The Freedmen's Association for the Relief of the Poor.*" " History does not afford a more striking illustration of Christian magnanimity."

NEGROES IN RICHMOND.—There are some twenty-five thousand coloured persons in Richmond. Between 6,000 and 7,000 are members in good standing of Christian churches, and nearly all attend services regularly. There are at least 200 men among this population who are worth from 2,000 dollars to 500 dollars, 200 who have property estimated at from 500 dollars to 5,000 dollars, and a number who are worth from 5,000 dollars to 20,000 dollars.—*From " Western Freedmen's Bulletin" for January,* 1864, *published at Chicago.*

PART II.

STATEMENTS IN PROOF OF
THE
INDUSTRIOUS CHARACTER
OF THE
FREEDMEN OF AMERICA,
OF THE
SUCCESS OF ENTERPRISES DEPENDENT ON THEIR WORK AS FIELD LABOURERS,
AND OF THE
GREAT IMPORTANCE, IN THIS CONNECTION, OF THE CO-OPERATIVE EFFORTS OF
FREEDMEN'S-AID ASSOCIATIONS
TOWARDS INCREASING FURTHER SUPPLIES OF COTTON FROM THE UNITED STATES.

FOR several of the subjoined facts, we are indebted directly or indirectly to the Official Report on the Freedmen of South Carolina to the Secretary of the Treasury, Washington; to the First and Second Annual Reports of the Education Commission for Freedmen, Boston, 1863, 1864; and to the First and Second Reports of the Freedmen's Inquiry Commission.

The subjoined Statement comprises also the testimony of official and other persons—American and English—most of them known to us as entirely unimpeachable witnesses.

But there is one illustration, which has often been referred to, of the industrial capacity of the Freed people (we do not need to restrict it to the Freed *men*), which, specially marked off by its own peculiar features and circumstances, deserves to be treated distinctly, and with at least sufficient detail to make its merits fairly understood.

We have before us four narratives of this experimental transaction, each one, we believe, entirely to be relied on; from which we collate and condense, as best suited to convey in nearly the words of the narrators a true and significant relation of it.

THE Sea Islands, so well known as those which give a name to the highest description of Cotton, fell into the hands of the Federal troops, November 14th, 1861.

The planters fled to the main, taking, as far as possible, their best field and house slaves, and leaving behind them 9,050 persons, a large proportion of whom were aged, infirm, and children. A good deal of corn and cotton fell into the hands of the Government—most of the cotton was unginned, some still on the stalk. The infirm class of labourers remaining on these 189 plantations were paid seemingly fair, but under the circumstances really meagre, wages. These were made even poorer when in a few cases base agents intervened. On December 16th, 1861 following, shipments of Cotton by the Government agent commenced, and, by June 13th, 1862, amounted to 1,166,330 lbs., leaving some more yet to be shipped. About one-half of it was ginned, some of which sold for 72 cents per ℔., and even more. The Government, encouraged by this industrial success, determined to plant a new crop for the season of 1862. The conducting of this work was entrusted to a Mr. Pierce, of Boston, who had been private Secretary to the Minister of the Treasury, and who had previously proved that he could turn to account the industry of the Contrabands—as the escaped slaves were then termed. But Mr. Pierce was no mere successful task-master; he seems, in truth, perhaps undesignedly, to have been if not a Founder yet a Pioneer of the Freedmen's-Aid Associations, and to have given their operations an important practical direction at the very outset. Roused by appeals from himself and another old friend of the present Chief-Justice Chase, and by those of General Sherman and Commander Dupont, a band of ladies and gentlemen and superintendents of industry, about 90 in number, gathered in Boston and New York. Philadelphia came in with a contribution of 6,000 dollars. With these and other contributions timely supplies were furnished, which, feeding the hungry, and clothing the naked, cheered the hearts of the blacks, strengthened also the hands of their white friends, and drew forth warm acknowledgments from Mr. Pierce and his coadjutors. Mr. Pierce received his commission in February, 1862; his first coadjutors, about fifty in number, landed at Beaufort on the 9th of March. Besides the teaching of the young, they directed their efforts to the promotion of self-respect and self-restraint, and the inculcation of lessons of morality and religion among all the people. The war had wrought evil work with them as well as with *all the appliances* needful for cultivating the soil. Instead of early February it was the last of March before the real work for raising the new crop began. Besides the delay, there were other difficulties to contend against. The Freedman's forethought was for the food of the next winter, and in that view he had been counselled by the soldiers who had lately quitted the Islands. The persuasion of the agents and teachers (most of them in all respects ladies and gentlemen) located on the 189 plantations of these swampy islands, was required to overcome the repugnance to the cultivation of Cotton—as recalling, if not renewing, to the Freedmen the reign of Slavery. But in spite of all difficulties, this population, not comprising more than 3,800 able-bodied men, had laboured so industriously, that in June, 1862, above 16,000 acres were bearing flourishing crops, giving an average of over four acres to every able-bodied man. 5480 acres were under Cotton 6 to 12 inches high, which at the end of the first season sufficed to pay the whole cost of the experiment. Corn enough for the community until the next harvest was also stored up, and the sum of 40,000 dollars clear profit paid into the United States Treasusy.—(Vide *Edinburgh Review*, Jan.—April, 1864, p. 229.) It is doubtful if this is not incorrect by one cipher too few, as it is stated in the Second Annual Report of the "Educational Commission of the New England Freedmen's-Aid Society," that the large sum derived by the Government from the sale of Cotton and other merchandise from the Sea Islands, amounted in January, 1863, to 422,000 dollars, over and above all expenses.

How these experiments of the working of 1862 affected both those who superintended and those by whose labour it was carried out, may be seen by the following Extract: —"The success of one of our Superintendents in conducting two of the largest plantations for the Government was so great, that he has, in connection with some friends at the North, purchased eleven plantations, comprising about 8000 acres, and is carrying them on this season by means of the old men, the women, and children,—most of the young and able-bodied men being now enlisted in the army of the United States."—*(First Annual Report of the Educational Commission for Freedmen.)*

This Agent, there is little doubt, was Mr. Philbrick, whose operations are reported in the next Annual Report as having raised, at "perhaps a little lower than the average former cost," and with this inferior labour—mainly of women, children, and old men—two-thirds of an ordinary crop. In the same year these blacks were making sales of minor market commodities to at least 150,000 dollars.

Then, as to the Freedmen themselves. At the end of the first year, at the sale which took place in March, 1863, four plantations, containing 3,500 acres, were bought by the Freedmen living upon them. At the sales of 1864, further tracts of land were purchased by them for about 40,000 dollars. *All these purchases were made from the savings of two years.*

In relation to these facts, the *North American Review* declared it could be claimed that the coloured population of the Sea Islands had been brought in two years from a state of utter destitution and ignorance to absolute prosperity and partial education, under all the disadvantages of military occupation and actual war, *by two comparatively feeble Societies in Boston and New York, aided by one in Philadelphia.*

It ought to be added that the Negroes of these Islands were regarded as the most "animalized" in all the United States, and their whole previous condition to have made up as desperate a case, for this kind of effort, as could well be conceived.

From the published letters of Joseph Simpson, Esq., of Manchester, we are enabled to give a confirmation, of a later date, of continued prosperity in these islands. Writing from Cincinnati, June 28th, 1865, he says:—

"One of the old slave-owners, Dr. Fuller, who held part of one of these very islands, accompanied the judge (Chase) thither, last month, in the full belief that his views as to Negro "incapacity," etc., would be confirmed. But after carefully examining all which had been done in the interim, he frankly confessed that he had never seen the land in better order, nor the people so happy and prosperous. His views were completely changed."

The experience of Colonel Eaton in the valley of the Mississippi, in one year only, speaks volumes in a few words. Grieved at the sufferings of the fugitive Negroes, he urged their claims upon General Grant, who, in consequence, appointed him General Superintendent of the Freedmen.

He arrived at Vicksburg, *August*, 1863, when the only industry among 20,000, was performed by twelve axes, and where such fearful scenes were to be witnessed as, he says, " were, if anything could do so, calculated to make one doubt the policy of emancipation."

By July 5th, 1864, 113,650 Freedmen had passed under his hands, of whom 10,500 only were not entirely self-supporting—but that number, including 7,200 who were old and young, crippled and sick, were employed either for prospective wages or for present relief in cultivating 5,500 *acres of Cotton,* and 1,300 acres in Corn and Vegetables, besides working at wood chopping. In all his district over 10,000 acres of cotton were under cultivation; some individual blacks managing as high as 300 to 400 acres.

And this great change, in one short year, had been effected mainly by the labours of Colonel Eaton, and a few noble co-workers—men and women sent out by a philanthropic Freedmen's-Aid Commission at Cincinnati.

We think the above case of the Sea Islands, and that of Colonel Eaton in the Mississippi, prove to demonstration the great value in an economico-industrial point of view, of the action and influences of Freedmen's-Aid Societies.

We are enabled from the Second Annual Report of the "New England Freedmen's-Aid Society," to give from the report of Mr. Yeatman, President of the Sanitary Commission, the following facts relating to the valley of the Mississippi:—

"General Thomas, in his report of the 15th October, 1863, states that fifteen coloured lessees had made cotton ranging from four to one hundred and fifty bales.

"Patrick (coloured), near Milliken's bend, made about twenty-seven bales, with six or seven persons to aid him.

"One hundred and fifty-three bales of cotton were raised at Goodrich's Landing, by twenty-two coloured men, who leased land and worked it on their own account. The average is seven bales; and one man raised forty-seven.

"Six negroes raised sixty-two bales—an average of twelve.

"At an average of 140 dollars (the net price paid for 101 bales, which had been sold), the proceeds of these bales would be 94,560 dollars, which would give each of the planters 2,300 dollars."

We are justified in stating that cases, similar in character and result to the above, might be cited as having occurred in several other Cotton States.

THE GAIN OF EMANCIPATION.

Hon. Joseph Segur, of Virginia, in a recent speech at Richmond, Virginia, declared that the Southern people were "inexpressible gainers by emancipation."

In the course of his remarks, he said:—" I speak from experience and observation. In my own country, where emancipation has been in practical operation from the commencement of the war, and on the Eastern shore of Virginia, where the policy has been fairly tested, it is an ascertained fact that the farmers make more clear money with hired coloured labour than they did when they cultivated the farms with their own slaves. The profit is generally doubled, sometimes trebled."—From the *Freedman*, December, 1865, New York, 61, Walker St.

ESTIMATED CHEAPNESS OF FREE LABOUR.

General Banks, who for a lengthened period was charged with the regulation of the Freedmen's condition in Louisiana during the war, in a lecture delivered at a meeting of a Young Men's Christian Association in the autumn of 1864, declared his belief that, under a well-established free labour system, Cotton might be grown at *very much lower prices* than by slaves.

It is a fact that twice in the decade ending about 1857 the crop of uplands Cotton had been sold for five cents per pound; and as we believe no one who will accept the teaching of experience doubts the greater cheapness of free labour, it does not seem unreasonable that a similar price, or one not exceeding eight cents, may obtain hereafter.

Anything that will accelerate the change from the present rates to prices like those now indicated, must be an immense gain to Lancashire and Great Britain generally, both in the economic and sanitary condition of all our people, and in a manufacturing and financial point of view.

It is a *moderate statement* to say that the *difference* between to-day's price of Cotton and that which may be certainly expected if a free labour system is soon established, is equal to the annual interest of our National Debt.

THE CHARACTER, WORK, AND RESULTS OF THE FREEDMEN'S-AID ASSOCIATIONS (OR COMMISSIONS).

The American Consul at Birmingham, has shown in a small naive narrative, called "How the Boys behaved," —and which he certifies as only simple truth—with what success the Negroes managed the properties abandoned to their care during the war. The effect of their conduct was to convince even *pessimist* planters from Mississippi, and another from Georgia, of the value of free labour, and to induce co-operation with the latter by some Manchester capitalists, for the purchase and cultivation of large Cotton estates.

A gentleman, sent out from Lancashire to inspect some enterprises of this kind, having discovered that he has the faculty of managing the coloured people in their new character of Freedmen, has returned to the United States to turn his ascertained power to his own account.

The importance of combining instruction and training with the relief of suffering and the supplies of material help, is recognized to be so great that it has become with the Freedmen's Commission an axiom never to be lost sight of—that the expenditure of 500 dollars in *absolutely needed supplies*, and 500 dollars for a Teacher-Agent, will go much farther, even in an economic point of view, than 1000 dollars all spent on the same community in measures of material aid.

It is not easy in a few words to state how in various ways this occurs, but we may supply one or two plain illustrations.

In not a few cases the Freedmen have refused to continue working on estates in the vicinity of which there were no schools, and both they and the planters are frequent in their applications to the Secretary of the Commission to have teachers sent to them. (The Freedmen of Louisiania have 144 schools, and entirely support the 139 teachers whom they engage.)

The Freedmen have been known to refuse entering into Contracts for labour until assured by their teachers that the Form of Contract was not a written instrument designed to re-enslave them.

One of the most important witnesses to whom we can refer in connection with this subject is Joseph Simpson, Esq., of Manchester, who, in the spring of 1865, accepted from the Central Committee of the Society of Friends for the Relief of the Emancipated Slaves of North America—an honorary Commission—to make a tour of investigation both as to the condition of the Freedmen and the work of the Associations in their aid.

This gentleman's sympathies had been avowedly on the side of the South, but it was only as a partisan of truth that he undertook a task which was neither without severe toil or peril to health.

After spending some months in various parts of the States, he writes, on his return to Manchester on September 9th, 1865, to sum up the results of his tour in the following terms:—

"And, speaking of the American Freedmen's-Aid Societies, I feel bound to state my conviction that better organisations do not exist anywhere than those of New York, Boston, Philadelphia, Baltimore, and Cincinnati. Of these I can speak from personal knowledge. Doubtless the same remark applies to others. During our "Cotton Distress" in Lancashire I acted on two working Committees for the distribution of funds amongst our mill "hands;" and I can safely say that neither in simplicity of organization, freedom from party bias, economy of working expenses, nor a conscientious desire to discharge a solemn duty in an honest, straightforward way, do the American Associations come one whit behind any Committee of which I have any knowledge. It is a noble sight to see the way in which men of all shades of religious and political belief (opulent business men and others) cheerfully unite in this work, sparing neither time, money, nor fatigue, in promoting the welfare of the Freedmen, which they deem a sacred trust. They feel that such a chance of doing good may never occur again; and now that they have got the small end of the wedge safely inserted, they mean to " drive it home " with all their might whilst opportunity offers.

"Already England has done much in this good work, and few things pleased me more in my travels than the oft-repeated expressions of gratitude to the " mother country " for her timely aid. I know that these thanks were sincere, and am equally satisfied that few things will tend more to bring the two great countries into that true concord which should ever exist between them, than such an evidence of brotherly sympathy as our English subscriptions would afford.

" And now, at the risk of repetition, I may state as the result of my observations—

" First,—That an almost incredible amount of destitution and misery prevails, and will continue to prevail, owing to the *disorganised condition* of society in the immense area over which the Freedmen are distributed, and the hostility of the Southerners to their former slaves.

" Second,—That as a rule the Freedmen are not only capable of sustained labour, but most desirous to obtain employment at equitable wages ; that they are *not idle* but *anxious to work.*

" Third,—That wherever schools have been established, the Freedmen, both young and old, have shown an extraordinary desire and capacity to learn.

" Fourth,—That the American Government is endeavouring, through the agency of the " Freedmen's Bureau," to protect and care for the millions of Freedmen so suddenly cast upon it.

"Fifth,—That the Christian population of the Northern States, through its various Freedmen's Aid Societies, are working with a zeal and energy which cannot be surpassed, to mitigate the distress, and to teach and enlighten the coloured population.

" Sixth,—That the sympathy and aid of the English people in this great work are most gratefully appreciated and have already done much to soften the hostile feeling which was engendered towards England during the war.

" And lastly,—That this sympathy and this aid are still imperatively required.

" The " Freedmen's Bureau " is increasing in efficiency every day, and labours diligently to suppress outrage and injustice towards the coloured people. Many good Abolitionists were at first inclined to question the usefulness of the Bureau. They feared it might be rendered comparatively useless by the trammels of official red-tapeism. But thanks to the wisdom and the energy of the head of the Department, General Howard, it is now doing a noble work, and daily proving a real blessing to those whose interests are committed to its keeping."

The following estimate of the result of free labour in the Southern States, from Messrs. Neill Brothers and Co.'s circular, dated New York, December 4, 1866, is most comprehensive and conclusive. It is an extract from the report of Major-General Sickles, commanding the department of the South, presented to Congress :—

"The misgivings of many planters as to the disposition of free negroes to work for wages gradually gave way. It soon became evident, that with proper energy, capital, patience, and tact on the part of the landholders, if they failed to make good crops, the failure would neither result from the lack of available hands, nor from the omission of the military authorities to exert a proper influence upon the labouring population.

"It is only just to declare, as the result of my observations, that the conduct of the coloured population has deserved all praise, and justifies the belief that, as Freedmen, they will become reliable, worthy, and useful citizens. And now, at the close of the year, I do not hesitate to affirm, that where the season has been favourable, wages liberal, facilities for culture ample, the superintendence diligent and judicious, and the labourers well treated, the average production has been equal to ordinary years before emancipation. 'Wherever the planters wish the thing to succeed, it is successful.'"

All General Sickles' antecedents make his testimony the more valuable.

Miss Elizabeth Jones, a teacher at Roanoke Island, North Carolina, who has been making an extensive tour on the mainland, reports much suffering among both white and coloured—a part the result of their own ignorance and folly, and a part the inevitable result of the habits of their former life. The old planters are often unable to secure profitable labour from their former slaves, and predict that they will fall away as the Indians have. She found, in Martin County, a Northerner who had purchased a farm, and commenced farming under the most unfavourable circumstances. It had been running wild during the war, was growing up to pine trees, fences destroyed, ditches filled up, &c. As he had built a steam mill by a gushing river, and was doing a good business there, he could not be present daily at his farm, so he hired an overseer, called the coloured ones together, and said : "I want labourers. I intend to cultivate so many acres in cotton. This man will oversee the work, not to oppress, but to encourage and direct. Those who work well shall be paid well. Those who do not will be immediately paid and discharged." The men were pleased, have done well, and are now picking such a crop of cotton as the astonished natives never saw before. They say, "The niggers will work for him because he is a Yankee."

Printed in Dunstable, United Kingdom